SISTER IN A PUZZLE

Sister In A Puzzle

DOMINIQUE LEONARD

ISBN-13: 979-8-218-72088-9
Printed in the United States of America

Contents

For my Little Bear,

May you exhibit compassion and understanding for others who may not look or behave the way that you do.

Prologue

He's waving goodbye to me, and we're all leaving his 30th birthday dinner. Today is a special day, a win. Jaivon has made it to year 30, yet I'm leaving this dinner feeling disheartened. There was something about his wave, the way he said "bye" to me as he drove off with his aide. Long and drawn out, slow. A reminder of his disability. I get home, and my heart feels a bit heavy. My husband and I pull into the driveway. I get out of the car, and I look at him while he's getting our son out of the car seat. All the built-up emotions start flowing from within me. I stand there, taking it all in. Emotions that have been building up for about fifteen years.

At this time, the feelings are all translating to a heavy sadness. "Babe, I'm gonna write a book about my life experience with my brother." I go into the house and head for the bathroom to gather my thoughts and shed some tears. My husband has no idea that I'm in the bathroom crying. He's getting things set up in the living room for us to watch the new Netflix show, "Forever," together. It was supposed to be an easy, lighthearted Friday. I knew I couldn't sit through the show without getting these thoughts off of my mind. I start to explain to him that I am feeling downhearted about my brother's condition. He reminds me that Jaivon may have his condition, but he does very well for himself. I want to share the source of the emotions that I experienced today with the entire world.

Chapter 1

The Yearning

"Mommy, Daddy, I want a sister!"

I never got one. It was always just Jaivon and I. His first words when I came home from the hospital were, "Take her back to the hospital." The toddler him said, "Take her back to the hospital." He was seven at the time that I was a newborn. I was constantly yearning for what we all know to be the "normal" sibling. You fight, but you love each other at the end of the night. You're plotting with each other when your parents turn their backs. You both come home from school and talk to each other about how your days were. Laugh together, watch a movie, and gain a deeper understanding of what happened in the film. That was not my experience growing up with Jaivon.

At times, it felt like I didn't even have a sibling. I'd walk past my brother's room, and he would turn his head the other way. I'd walk past his room and see him rocking back and forth, humming some song. Sometimes, he'd catch me staring at him rocking from the crack of his door, and he'd immediately stop and stare back. Almost as if he's saying, "And what are you looking at me for? Can't you see I'm rocking?" Sometimes, I'd be bold and open his door and go into his room. I hoped that he would embrace me and want to spend time with me. Instead, it was "get out". However, there were times when he would embrace me with a smile and start laughing, and I decided to come into his room. You see, with Jaivon, everything depended on his mood. With his condition, his mood could switch in a heartbeat, and unfortunately, a simple mood switch could make our days take a turn for the worse. However, even when he was in a cheerful mood, the conversations were not what I had hoped for. In my head, I'd walk into his room, and we would start chatting it up like regular siblings. Instead, when we were conversing, I was leading the conversation. He would generally respond to what I was saying, perhaps asking how my day was.

Other than that, our conversations in his room were very dull. I hate to call them boring, but I don't know how else to describe them. His mind wasn't mentally in the space to hold a conversation exciting enough to entertain a younger sibling.

I used to wonder if he didn't like me and why. Or at least it came across as dislike due to the way he behaved towards me at times. I felt that he disliked me because of the way he would straight-up ignore me when I walked past his door. I mean, I could say something as simple as "Hey Jaivon," and depending on his mood, sometimes I wouldn't get a response. I know you heard me loud and clear, Jaivon. Being ignored would hurt my feelings because I didn't know what I ever did to him. When I would bring it up to my mom, she would tell me to leave him alone; it was part of his condition. Although he was in the house, I would feel so alone sometimes. It didn't make matters better that Mommy continued to chalk it up to his condition when I could complain to her about being ignored by him.

At some point, my parents considered adopting a child. Is it because I wanted a sibling besides Jaivon, or are there personal reasons they never told me?

Anywho, we found an adoption agency and ended up in a meeting to learn about the process. I was so excited at that meeting. The woman in charge explained the process of adopting a child and outlined all the details involved. I remember the three of us looking on their website at the kids that were up for adoption. My mom made it very clear she did not want a baby, and she did not want a teenager. It felt as if we were online shopping for my sister. I was thrilled to finally have the chance to have the engaging, interactive sibling I had always yearned for. I am finally getting a sister! Unfortunately for me, they never went through with it. I came to terms with the fact that I wasn't getting the sister I wanted. Acceptance. Something I became very familiar with in my childhood.

Then, there were the outbursts. Lord have mercy; these outbursts have caused me trauma and anxiety. I still, to this day at 23 years old, replay the outbursts in my head. I hear his screams, his extreme raging. As I grew older, I could sense when he was about to explode. My stomach would start to turn, and I would be so nervous to the point where I had to poop. To this day, if I am in a room where a confrontation is happening, I get that same anxious feeling in my stomach. It's a reminder of what I dealt with growing up. At least when my parents were still married, Daddy was at home to protect Mommy. And although after their divorce, Daddy was nothing short of involved in my life, he couldn't be there to protect mommy in the house.

My childhood with a sibling like Jaivon has been eventful, with both good and bad times. It's been an emotional roller-coaster for our entire household. I thank God for giving our family light at the end of the tunnel, but boy, oh boy, that tunnel has been long and dark.

Chapter 2

Psychotic Break
#1

I was in kindergarten when I witnessed my first psychotic break from Jaivon. I was five years old, and Jaivon was twelve. That means we're seven years apart. I don't even remember what triggered it. I remember we were all sitting in the kitchen, and he just started raging out. Screaming at the top of his lungs, and he threw a glass cup in the direction that I was sitting. It all happened so fast. I was sitting there, watching the commotion and observing. Mommy probably told him no to something. That's what triggered many of his outbursts when we were younger. He wouldn't get his way with something, and he'd flip. These outbursts were no temper tantrums now. These were violent, extreme outbursts. Dangerous. Scary. To the point where Mommy knew she needed to seek outside help but couldn't seek it from the police.

Police officers are not trained to understand mental illness. They are trained to understand violence and threats to society. Violence means pulling the trigger or even killing. As he got older, the outbursts only got worse. He was becoming stronger.

That night, when I'm sure we all thought it was over and he was calm, I heard my mom go into his room to tell him to go to bed. Most normal boys would comply, turn off the lights, and call it a night. Maybe they would roll their eyes when their mom closed the room door and start pretending to sleep with the covers over their heads. That night, Jaivon was not ready to go to sleep. He was rocking, a habit he typically exhibited while listening to music. He would sit crisscrossed in his bed or on the floor, hands on his elbows, and rock while humming to whatever music was playing in his headphones.

Mommy wanted him to go to bed, and when she went into his room, I just heard loud screaming. I see my mom come out of his room after the "earthquake" with blood running down her chest and her shirt torn. He bit her. Jaivon was a biter at one point during his earthquakes. Getting bitten by a twelve-year-old is not the same as getting bitten by a teething infant. Your flesh will bleed, and the skin will more than likely come off. Next thing you know, the ambulance is pulling up to take them to the hospital. Jaivon spent two nights away at a mental institution. Mommy and Daddy went to visit him both days, but I don't think they wanted to bring me there. I didn't even realize the severity of what happened that night.

The first outburst was the first of many violent episodes that I would see and hear in my lifetime. It is truly a "you just had to be there" kind of experience that I will do my best to describe. Little did I know at the time that this was the beginning of the trauma that I would embark on as a child and later on as a young adult. Notice how I referenced his outburst as an earthquake? Whenever there's an earthquake, the average person typically tries to take shelter. They'll hide under a table or underneath something sturdy so that nothing falls on them and injures them. Well, that was me during Jaivon's outbursts. Little me would hide in the closet, my "shelter," and wait for it to be over. I would be so terrified and just hoping that it would be over as soon as possible. I heard yelling, screaming, and loud thumping on the floor. Things sounded as if they were getting thrown across the room at times. I could listen to the damage and destruction that was being done right across the hall from my room.

I would sit in the closet, knees folded into my chest, just hoping that everyone would be okay—especially Mommy, as she was the main target during Jaivon's earthquakes. After Jaivon's violent outbursts, he would sometimes burst into tears and start sobbing. He appeared to feel a sense of remorse, perhaps even regret. I always hated watching him in this state because he was genuinely so sorrowful. When he would be in this depressed state, he looked like such a child. Snot would be running down his nose, and he would be going on about how sad he was. He would sit on his bed, "boo-hoo," crying intense tears. It was heartbreaking to watch. Granted, these extreme lows happened after he hurt someone or damaged objects in the house, but my heart still felt for him.

There were times when my brother would finally calm down from his episode, and Mommy would give him Benadryl to help him relax, and he would go straight to sleep. The silence in the house when Jaivon was finally asleep after an eventful night was impeccable. We always appreciated it when the earthquake was over.

The next day, my dad drove me to school. There was a song playing on the radio, and although I don't remember the name of it, I remember that song to the tee. I could identify it if I heard it again. But I correlate that song with what I could remember from my first time seeing Jaivon explode. That is how much of a scar that first psychotic break has left on me. Every part of it remains in my memory, including the day that followed. I just witnessed something the average 5-year-old doesn't usually witness on a school night, yet I still had to show up to school and be a student. I remember describing to all my friends what had taken place the night before. Of course, none of them could relate, and this used to drive me crazy as a kid.

Chapter 3

"No one understands me"

"No one understands me". I would constantly feel this as I was growing up with Jaivon. I desperately wanted a friend who could relate to me—someone who walked a mile in my shoes. However, I never had it, and to this day, I still don't have anyone in my circle who can relate to what I experienced growing up with Jaivon. I remember one night, my mom sat me down and gave me this book about having a sibling with autism. Mommy always wanted to make sure that I became educated on a situation, and she still does the same thing today. She wants me to be knowledgeable about what is at hand before me. In this case, Mommy wanted me to look at what other siblings feel that are in my shoes. I suppose she wanted me to know that there were others like me out there:

living in a household where a brother or sister is not what we know to be "normal."

I know she meant well, but this book did nothing for me. I didn't even want to open it. The topic of my brother was always sensitive back then, and it still is sometimes to this day in my adulthood. Tears came to my eyes, and I remember crying out to my parents. "No one understands what this feels like. You guys both have normal siblings, and you don't get it".

I would try ranting to my mom when Jaivon was doing something that would irritate me. There would be times when she didn't want to hear it. I'm sure she was already overwhelmed and overstimulated with her day, and then here I came to tell her about how her son was bothering me. "Don't you know he has a problem, Dominique? He has a problem!". I would cry to myself every time she said this. It was a reminder that my brother wasn't normal, and he never would be. I would also feel guilty for upsetting Mommy. I would think about everything that she is already going through having a son with special needs. These are the terms I must accept. I'm not saying I had to tolerate him getting on

my nerves or occasionally ignoring me, but I needed to ac-
knowledge that Jaivon was different from me.

After Jaivon's explosion when I was five, none of my
friends could relate to what I had just witnessed inside of
my house that night. I remember telling them about it, and
they were just in awe. One of my friends said she'd beat him
up for me. Little did I let her know that she wouldn't stand
a chance. Especially not when he is in his unstable, raging
mode. Although I wanted to very badly, I knew no one with
a brother like mine. This was frustrating because, despite my
repeated explanations of what goes on in our household, no
one could understand. Being a great listener is a skill that
every human being should learn. But physically, being able to
understand is a gift that only those who have been in your
situation possess. People can empathize and sympathize, but
not everyone can understand. That's what I was looking for:
understanding. Everyone got to go home to their normal siblings and go to school with them. I longed for the "regular"
sibling dynamic for a very long time.

I often felt that my friends took their siblings for granted.
Truly. They'd talk about how their brothers or sisters were
so annoying or how they'd get on their nerves. In my head,

I would think, well, at least you have a sibling who gets on your nerves. At times, I felt like an only child. I'd think to myself, "I want a sibling who gets on my nerves sometimes, but we still love each other at the end of the night." Of course, Jaivon was living in the house with me, but we didn't bond. I could talk to Mommy about how I felt, and Daddy too. But they pretty much just chalked it up to there's nothing we can do about him being that way; he has a condition. Little Dom just had to deal with it. I had to accept the reality: Jaivon isn't going to change. So, there I was, continuing to live life as usual alongside my brother, who would call me "Pauline Curtis" for no reason.

Chapter 4

Pauline Curtis

Who on earth is Pauline Curtis? That was me. Jaivon had pet names for certain people, and that just happened to be mine. This name would get under my skin. I can laugh about it now, looking back, but at the moment, it would make my blood boil. "Mommy, Jaivon keeps calling me Pauline Curtis!" "Just ignore him, Dominique". "Just ignore him" seemed to be the trending word of advice. That could be another way of saying he has a condition and I need to work on accepting it. I couldn't just ignore this behavior. It's so irritating, and that's not my name! Jaivon loved Barney as a kid. There were two kids on the show: One's name was Pauline, and the other was Curtis. He put the two together and made it my nick-name.

It's very ironic yet creative. I applaud you for your creativity, Jaivon. Sometimes, he would call me that name jokingly or with the straightest face. Boy, oh boy, it would PISS ME OFF! He knew it, too. That's one thing about Javivon; he knew how to get on your nerves. He'd do it on purpose, too. Jaivon can be described in many ways, but "dumb" or "oblivious" is not one of them. He knew exactly what he was doing when he would call me Pauline freaking Curtis. He knew it got under my skin, and he continued to do it. It was like a game to him. Jaivon knew how to play mind games, and sometimes, it worked to his advantage. He often got what he wanted as a result of his mind games. Fortunately, he outgrew this phase, but man, it was rough ignoring that one. Mommy's pet name was "Darling." Or "darling, darling baby." Only when he was mentally stable. When he was unstable, mommy was "Bitch".

Chapter 5

The Other Sister

Jaivon and I don't share the same father, and he has another sister on his dad's side named Layana. I have seen her one time in my entire life. She came to visit him at our grandmother's house in Boston. Boston was her and their dad's hometown, as well as Jaivon and I's grandparents' hometown. Jaivon and I would go to Boston every Summer with our mom and stay with our grandparents when she was working. I think Layana is my age. Maybe she's older than me? Possibly closer to Jaivon's age? Anywho, when Jaivon would get into his psycho moments, he would tell me I'm not a good sister and that he likes Layana better.

You could only imagine how this made me feel as a little girl. I'd ask myself what I ever did that was so wrong to him. First of all, Layana was never an active family member in his life, so there is no way he could prefer her over me. I would reason with myself that he couldn't possibly think she is a better sister than I am. I would think to myself, "She doesn't even call you. She doesn't even make an effort to come by and see you when we're in Boston. You barely even know her". Adult me wonders what it's like having a sibling with special needs that you know is out there but have no bond with. You know he exists, but you don't call or text. You really could care less. Or maybe Layana does care about Jaivon; I can't say. There was a time when I, as a little girl, would hope that she could be our sister. Goodness, I was so desperate for a sister at the time. I wonder if she thinks about him or wants to know him. Layana, if you're reading this, call your brother and check on him. I don't think he's heard from you in the past decade or longer.

Maybe Layana is just like her and Jaivon's dad. Absent and carefree. "Not my problem" mindset. This mindset makes me sad to think about because family is supposed to love you, regardless of mental illness. I am not implying that Layana and their father don't love Jaivon. However, he hasn't received the love he deserves. Where were they when Jaivon graduated high school? We had family fly in from out of the United States to see him graduate, but they couldn't catch a flight from Boston. Where were they on the birthdays? Even if a plane ticket was not feasible at the time, why are the phone calls still not made to this day? The check-ins? The simple "I love you" messages and reminders.

Chapter 6

The Aides

Aides. These were the people that would come into our house and make my mom's life ten times easier. The aides were exactly as they sounded. They were an aide to our family and a great help to my mom and brother. Their sole purpose was to focus specifically on my brother's needs. They would take him to and from wherever he needed to go and provide physical support for him. They'd make sure he did his homework back when he was in school. The aides would even help him make his food or take him to fun extracurricular places. I used to want an aide as a kid, although there was nothing wrong with me. All I saw was him with someone who was there to focus solely on him and take him to fun places. Of course, as a kid, I wanted this. Who wouldn't?

I remember he had one particular female aide who I took up to my room and asked her to play with me. In my head, I finally had a prominent sister figure. At the end of the night, Mommy and Daddy reminded me that she was not there for me but for Jaivon only. Bummer.

Don't get me wrong, Jaivon may have had aides, but that didn't mean that he was incapable of carrying out daily functions. He is very competent and also physically able. His competence is something for which we, as a family, are deeply grateful. Although his mental capacity is not where a "normal" thirty-year old mans' is, we thank God that he can walk, talk, articulate his needs clearly, and perform daily functions. There have been over ten aides coming into our home to help with Jaivon. My mom would get them through an agency. He also had behavioral specialists who would come in, along with counselors. Of course, at that point, I also wanted a counselor.

Little me just wanted a buddy in the house because I always felt as if I didn't have one. He has had some interesting aides come through, and the most interesting was a lady named Tika. Tika was a kind, middle-aged African woman. She was punctual to work and genuinely cared about Jaivon.

However, she was constantly praying because, according to her Islamic beliefs, she had to pray five times a day toward Mecca. She would always let us all know when she was about to go and pray. She'd say, "I'm going to go do my prayers." And she'd disappear into the upstairs office and lay out her rug and take out this necklace. She'd start off standing, then bow down. She'd sit as well at some point; I mean, it was a whole routine. I wonder if Jaivon was ever triggered by her abruptly leaving to go pray every time she was working with him.

There was always a "honeymoon phase" with every aide. This phase was the point in time when the aides had not yet witnessed an earthquake. You see, Jaivon is very respectful and has excellent manners when he is himself. It's almost what some would consider "cute," even though he's a grown man. But when that switch goes off in his head, that Jaivon that we all know is gone and nowhere to be found. Some of the aides are taken aback by the switch that goes off in his head, causing him to explode. Unfortunately for Tika, their honeymoon phase was over. It was nice while it lasted, but every aide eventually came to the end of this phase. This time, when he flipped, Mommy wasn't the prime target. It was Tika. I remember coming home and hearing that Jaivon had punched Tika in the jaw and as a result of this, her dentures were broken. After that, I saw Tika maybe a few more times, and then she quit. She said she was moving to Africa. Maybe she did. Perhaps she didn't. I would leave, too, after that.

I'm sure that most of his aides who quit were sick of Jaivon and his shenanigans. I would be, too. It takes a lot of patience to work with someone like Jaivon when he is unstable. When he's stable, working with him is a breeze because he does so much for himself. It was time to find another aide. I know my mom was overwhelmed, but she never quit on him. When an aide would call out unexpectedly, it would trigger Jaivon. From the moment my mom told him they would not be able to make it, there was a chance he would flip. Through all of the aides, he had one that I took a strong liking to. His name was Kenny. Kenny worked with Jaivon for a year or two, and he was like another brother to me. I mean, he was hilarious, truly. I remember he told me before: "Dominique, I wish I could be your aide even though there's nothing wrong with you." And then my brother started to show his darker colors to Kenny. I don't want to call that side his "true colors" because that dark side is not who Jaivon truly is as a person.

"Snoop Dog". That's how it all started. That was Jaivon's pet name for Kenny: "Snoop Dog". As I mentioned before, mine was "Pauline Curtis". No exaggeration. Every pet name Jaivon gives is strategic. I have a feeling that Kenny was "Snoop Dog" because he had a tall and slim build that favored the real "Snoop Dog". I remember that day Daddy was at the house. Mommy was out of town working. She owns an NCLEX® prep company and would travel back and forth to Boston to teach classes. This is how we ended up there every Summer with her. I don't remember what triggered Jaivon, but the next thing I knew, he was outside our house, exploding. Mind you, we live in a predominantly white neighborhood in one of the whitest cities. I don't mean to make this about race, but that's just the reality.

When you are one of the only black families in the neighborhood, attention is easily drawn to you. Especially if a grown black man is lashing out at the house. And here we are, the family with the young man outside screaming at the top of his lungs, cursing. I don't even know what triggered him. I remember looking outside from my bathroom and seeing him circling Kenny's car. Kenny was circling behind him to make sure Jaivon didn't do anything crazier than the crazy he was already doing. By that, I mean breaking a car window or something. It wasn't above Jaivon to do that when he was unstable. He cannot think clearly or logically when he is having a psychotic outbreak. We pray for the best and hope it ends soon when it does happen. At this moment outside, I kid you not, he was foaming at the mouth.

Lo and behold, Jaivon decides to call our grandmother on the phone. "Grandma!" And he proceeded to tell her what was wrong. This was an ongoing trend that happened for all of Jaivon's outbursts for the longest time. My grandmother was very accusatory to my mother because she was only hearing her precious autistic grandson's side of the situation. As a child, I desperately wanted my brother to flip in front of my grandparents. I wanted him to scream and cuss and be violent in front of them. I wanted them to see the dark side of Jaivon so they could stop assuming that precious Jaivon would never do the things that we described. Jaivon didn't flip in front of them for years. But when it finally did, you can be sure that I was satisfied. I know my mom was, too.

There were probably times when she felt misunderstood, having to explain Jaivon's earthquakes to others constantly. When someone finally witnessed it, she didn't have to work as hard explaining it because they'd physically experienced it. Finally, Jaivon calms down and comes back inside of the house. I'm just glad it's over, and I'm sure Kenny is fed up and ready to go home. He was always very patient with Jaivon, though.

Then there was Larissa. He developed an extreme fondness for his aide, Larissa. Larissa was very good to Jaivon. She genuinely cared about him and seemed enthused to see and work with him. She would take him out all the time, and many of the locations consisted of food places. Mommy had to tell Larissa to cut down on this. She even had to tell Larissa not to bring her outside food to the house because it would encourage Jaivon to want some, and Jaivon needed to eat a bit healthier.

At the time, he was starting to experience outbursts, with the source of anger being food aggression. For example, wanting Subway and not getting the green light from Mommy would trigger an outburst. Sometimes, even his wanting Taco Bell and getting a "no" from my mom would trigger an outburst. Therefore, we didn't need him seeing any outside food coming into the house. The goal was always to minimize the triggers. Larissa had an incredible streak with

Jaivon. She worked with him for multiple years. She would take him skating every weekend with no hesitation. Skating every weekend was a part of Jaivon's routine, and it still is. He truly loves it, and he's very skilled at it. Jaivon can skate for real, okay? Please don't read this thinking because he has a mental illness; he's skating at the skating rink slowly and abnormally. My guy skates on the outside with the fast people, okay. Mommy even bought him a pair of lit-up skates. Although he had his pair of skates, he never wore them. He was spending money every week to rent skates, which was a waste. Now that I look back, I know she meant well, but I can understand why he didn't want to wear them. I don't know any normal male our age who is going to wear light-up skates. None of those guys at the skating rink wear light-up skates; they're all plain black.

I remember there was a time when Larissa was ready to leave the skating rink, but Jaivon didn't want to, so they stayed for hours more. I wonder if she did this because she didn't want him to flip. What do you do in that situation? At the time, we lived about forty minutes from the skating rink. I wonder if he could've flipped in the car if they left early when he didn't want to. I guess we'll never know. When Larissa gave her notice that she would not be returning to work with Jaivon, he was devastated. He loved Larrisa. My mom has used her recently to help with Jaivon for backup coverage when his aides couldn't make it.

There have been great aides, and there have been bad aides. The custom of having an aide in the house was just standard for all of us. He has always had one for as far back as I can remember. Mommy always went above and beyond to ensure that Jaivon was supported adequately in every aspect. However, some people in our lives wanted to help him a bit too much.

Chapter 7

Jaivon, The Twenty-Year Old Baby

Grandma and her sister, my great aunt Cheryl, are coming to town. That means Jaivon will not only behave, but he's liable to be babied. My grandparents and great-aunt would baby the heck out of Jaivon. One day, while they were in town, we had a family function at the house. There's food, a good amount of people, and everyone's talking and having a good time amongst one another. Suddenly, I look over, and something catches my attention negatively. I kid you not; my brother, who was about twenty years old at the time, was sitting on Cheryl's lap. Are my eyes deceiving me? I am not even sitting on Aunt Cheryl's lap at this point, and I'm seven years younger than Jaivon. What made her want a grown, big-behind man to sit on her lap? It's because Jaivon was not a typical adult to many in our family. He had a pass for a good amount of things, and I guess lap sits at the time were one of those passes, but why?

I always wanted my brother to have a sense of normalcy. I didn't want him to be treated differently because of his condition. But he was by Aunt Cheryl and my grandparents. Their behavior, in my opinion, wasn't nipped in the bud when he was a child, so it just continued through his adulthood—making me sick. Jaivon is sitting on Aunt Cherly's lap and it wasn't his idea. It was Cheryl's. I don't know what she was thinking. "Come, JJ, sit on my lap." And he sits on her lap! He doesn't do it because he's mentally ill and cannot think for himself. He proceeds to do it because he knows he has her tricked right where he wants her. He's playing her, and she's unknowingly letting him.

Mommy sees this and tells him to get up. On that same trip, Aunt Cheryl brought Jaivon this hat that had to have been for a five-year-old. It's a stuffed animal hat. In her defense, many teenagers were wearing similar hats at the time, but they had a knitted design (much different). Knitted hats with an animal figure, not a physical animal for a hat.

She meant well, but it still upsets me. I'm so angry that this is how she views my brother. As a child, although he is physically an adult. My mom and I crack up about this ridiculous-looking hat. There have been moments where all we can do is laugh. Taking everything seriously will physically harm you. We're laughing it off, but I know deep down we are both frustrated by this behavior. I believe that every adult, regardless of their mental capacity, should be treated their age. Of course, within reason. There were times when Jaivon would struggle to cut his pancakes when we ate out at a breakfast restaurant. The concept of holding the fork into the pancake and using the knife to cut was just a fine motor skill that wasn't clicking. Someone would cut the pancakes for him, and if it were up to me, I would let him figure it out. Every person can learn and increase knowledge through the act of practicing a skill. A skill that someone else completes for us constantly will never be perfected.

When the three of us would travel to Boston every Summer for Mommy's job, the time to go back to reality always came quickly. When it was finally time for us to go back home, Grandma would give Jaivon "the talk." Every. Single. Time. She would tell him to make sure he doesn't act up when we get back to Georgia. He would promise her every single time that he would behave. Although I knew these talks were pointless, a part of me still held on to the hope that Jaivon would keep his word. He never did. Back to Georgia, back to earthquakes.

Chapter 8

Daddy

Jaivon and I don't share the same dad. I believe that this has caused a lot of jealousy on Jaivon's end. Because of his condition, he doesn't process emotions the same way that we do. A simple "I miss you" phone call to your real dad when you miss them or haven't seen them is the action of a normal person. Some "normal" people say screw it and chalk it up to having daddy issues. Some guys know it's their dad's loss for not wanting to be involved and end up becoming mama's boys. Others hold a grudge and resent their fathers, causing relationship issues with women. For Jaivon, these feelings of neglect trigger his earthquakes or outbursts. He is not normal.

Daddy (my Daddy) has been in Jaivon's life since he was two. Jaivon has never attacked Daddy. I don't even think he would attack his father. There's just something special about having a male presence in the house. That's how things were intended to be from the beginning of time. Now, I can't tell the story from my parents' perspective, only mine.

I remember feeling like Jaivon just disliked me. The way he'd ignore me or not want to be bothered with me was just so abnormal. You don't act that way towards the sister that you love, right? One day, I asked him. I asked him if he didn't like me because he was jealous that I had my dad. "That's correct," was his response. Through all of this, Mommy, Daddy, Jaivon, and I would still go on family outings, just like any normal family. We would go skating once a week every week at our local skating rink. We went on vacations together, whether it was the four of us or just Mommy, Jaivon, and I. Daddy would get up in the morning and cook breakfast for the entire household. He would play "Breezin" by George Benson and set the mood for the morning. We could all smell the eggs, turkey bacon, and his special cream of wheat from upstairs. Everyone looked forward to Daddy's breakfasts during the school week. Especially Mommy because she didn't have to get the kids up for school. She had home-cooked porridge, hot and ready in bed.

I know that Daddy loves Jaivon. But there's nothing like a father's love for his son. Jaivon never experienced that. His father wasn't involved at all. I can probably count on ten fingers the amount of times that I've seen Jaivon's dad in my twenty-three years of life. That's just sad. Jaivon has only ever lived with my mom. His dad has never kept him for the entire Summer or anything like that. He'd buy him birthday gifts or let him spend the night at his house once every seven to ten years, but that's about it. I hate that my brother had that experience with his father. I know it bothered him deep down inside because a lot of times when he was getting ready to explode, he would mention his dad. Should that tell us that he associates his father with feelings of anger?

I remember standing in the kitchen with my mom and Jaivon one day. We're getting ready to go to school, and it's time for Jaivon to get on the bus to school. The bus would pull up in front of our house. He rode what ignorant people would call the "short bus." A bus that's not made as long and intended for mentally or physically disabled students. I could feel it in my stomach that his behavior was off that morning. When he started calling his dad's number and left him a voicemail, I knew it was coming soon. "Hey, dog. Can you buy me a CD and make sure that 'Birthday Sex' is on it?" My mom and I both looked at each other and shook our heads in unison. The look we'd give each other when we could feel him starting up. In those moments with Mommy and I, what was understood didn't need to be said. The song 'Birthday Sex' by Jeremih was a bit mature for Jaivon at the time, so Mommy would tell him not to play it. Would you believe that during some of his episodes, he would blast 'Birthday Sex' at the highest volume to piss my mom off? The adult me could laugh, but the kid me wanted to know what in the world was happening.

Daddy came to Mommy's rescue for all of Jaivon's earthquakes. I remember hearing Jaivon start screaming and cursing, accompanied by loud thumps against the floor in his room next to mine. Here we go, time to prepare for impact and take shelter. My mom would yell, "Ta!" and my dad would come to save the day. He would handle Jaivon the way any honest man or father would. Some may call it insensitive. I don't care. If they weren't in our household, the opinions mean nothing. One day, Mommy and Jaivon were in the office room, the day after Jaivon's 8th grade dance. It is a day so special that you would think he would be coming down from cloud nine the day after. Something triggered Jaivon, and my mom was sitting in her high chair at her desk on her computer. Her computer desk was right next to the window. Measuring from the ground up, this window was taller than mommy. It was not short in length and her whole body could fit through it if she wanted it to for whatever reason. Something triggered my brother, and he pushed my mom's chair with all his force toward the window. Thankfully, my mom hit the wall next to the window. Do you know what's liable to happen when a 170-something-pound woman is pushed with force against a glass window? Yeah, she can fall out and plummet to her death. Daddy was infuriated, as any father would be. He picked Jaivon up and slammed him to the ground. The wind was knocked out of him.

My mom could have died a very tragic death if she had fallen out of the window and gone too soon. You would be hearing it in the news: "Local black Georgia woman, dead at 40 after mentally unstable son pushes her out of the window". Everyone would've been saying why didn't somebody do something? Crying at her funeral that she was gone too soon. How do you really "punish" a son with Jaivon's circumstances for this deed? Do you take away his electronics and all of his favorite devices? In his case, it would be his CDs and CD player. Do you not let him leave the house for extracurriculars (no skating)? Do you use physical correction?

At this age, he's past whoopings. The course of action for consequences was up to Mommy and Daddy at this point, and I don't question their methods in this situation. Neither should anyone who is not living this life or parenting a mentally ill son with psychotic breaks.

Chapter 9

Jaivon, The Gifter, The Scholar

Regardless of the circumstances, Jaivon is a brilliant man. His personality is charming, and it is an honor to know him and call him not only a brother but a friend. He is kind, polite, and always thinks of those he loves. He responds with "please" and "no thank you" when speaking to others. Jaivon enjoys laughing at the little things, and when he gets to cracking up, it lights up the world of those around him. When he starts talking about music, you can see the passion in his eyes as he lights up, elated to be discussing his gift. He sets up his DJ equipment and MC's the family events with all of the latest music, and even old-school tunes. He uses his laptop and a professional mixer to transition each song in a way that flows seamlessly. The way he dances when he hears music that he likes just tugs on the heartstrings of those around him and draws them to the dance floor.

He graduated high school with a regular high school diploma, not a GED. His graduation day was a fantastic day for our family, and I know it meant the world to my mom. Mommy has done it. She has accomplished what every mother wants to see her child do: graduate from high school and receive their diploma. The entire family wore blue, matching his cap and gown outfit. It was a fun-filled day, and we all got to see Jaivon achieve something that some "normal" people don't even reach. He earned that diploma on his own, and we are all so proud of him for it. After high school, Mommy wanted the next big thing for Jaivon. She started by letting him move from his room upstairs into the basement of our home. The basement had recently been redone into a one-bedroom, one-bathroom apartment, so Jaivon had his own space down there. I loved this for him because he was developing into a grown man, and at some point, he needed to begin making the transition to becoming more independent. Mommy was ready for Jaivon to do more. She never wanted Jaivon to sit and stare at the wall just because of his condition. So, college it was, but with a twist.

Mommy found Jaivon a live-in center for adults with special needs, helping them gain a sense of independence and experience a replica of college life. After what felt like a two-hundred-page application, Jaivon was accepted into 'Cave Springs.' He was so thrilled to be moving out of the house for the first time on his own. He would have a roommate and get to truly live independently. It was almost like a dorm setup, with a common area where everyone could hang out and a laundry room where individuals could wash and dry their clothes. He was on the phone, telling everyone, "I'm going to college!" Mommy would smile at hearing this. It truly brought her joy to hear him expressing his excitement to everyone on the phone that he was going to what he knew to be college. When people would ask, "What college are you going to?" He would respond with "Cave Springs". Although we all knew it was not an actual college, the family was pleased that he was ecstatic to be moving on to the next chapter in his life.

Unfortunately, the school's system only allows students to live there for a year. But it was so nice while it lasted and a breath of fresh air for both of us. Mommy would have kept him there longer if that was an option. Possibly even permanently. Aside from graduating high school and moving on afterward, Jaivon has always had a true passion for music. He LOVES music with everything in him. Anytime a new song comes out, he's the first to hear it. We'd be driving in the car together, and a song would come on on the radio, and he'd say, "I got that song! Do you know this song, Dominique? I got this song on my phone." He'd ramble about how much he likes the song, tell me who it's by, ask me if I've ever heard it before, and let me know maybe two to three times that he has the song on his phone. He comes from a time when CDs were the primary source of music, accompanied by CD players. He has had hundreds, I mean hundreds, of CDs in his room. He would download music to the CDs and burn them for himself and others.

You know that Jaivon loves you if he burns you a CD. He downloads the music and sits there, transferring it to the CD. Then, in all caps, in a thick black Sharpie, he'll write your name on the CD and give it to you. As I'm writing this book, I realize that CD gifting was one of his love languages. He would custom-make CDs with certain tracks for the people he loves. Our entire immediate family has received one from him, and I know that if I go outside and look in my car right now, I can find a CD that Jaivon has made for me. Gosh, he is so talented and also patient because I'm not about to sit there and burn a whole CD. Another one of Jaivon's gifts for those that he loves is a t-shirt. Anytime we would go out of town with Mommy, he just had to bring back a t-shirt for every single aide. Oh my goodness, even if he had brought back a t-shirt before from the same place, he had to get one again. But that's Jaivon for you. He's thoughtful, and he's considerate of the people he loves. To this day, he still sends us birthday cards when he can.

He is also a gentleman. When we all go out to eat together, Jaivon makes it his business to hold the door open for everyone. He's learning that that's what you do for a lady, and I don't remember the last time I opened my door when going out to eat with Jaivon. Before we even get to the door, he says, "I got the door," and he marches to the door, making sure that he is the one that gets to it first so that he can open it. He always blesses his food and volunteers to bless the food when we have dinner as a family. The traits he exhibits are those of a kind, caring, and selfless man whom I am blessed to call my brother. His mental illness has not stopped him from displaying the characteristics that make him a phenomenal person.

Chapter 10

Mexico

Mexico. That word sends a chill up our spines. What was meant to be a fun-filled family vacation turned out to be a horror story and nightmare with Jaivon. His outbursts always remained in the walls of our house. Jaivon never acted up in public; he just didn't. He knew better. He had some common sense and a conscience that knew lashing out in public was just not socially acceptable until he didn't. Mommy planned a vacation to Cancun, Mexico, for her, Jaivon, and me—a mother planning a vacation to spend time with her kids soaking up the sun. We had a great time. We checked into our hotel and received wristbands that indicated our ages. We rode the tour bus around the resort, took a significant number of photos, and shared many laughs. One day, we went out on Main Street, and Jaivon wanted to eat at Subway. We were walking into the store, and Mommy told Jaivon, 'No subway.'

We were staying at a hotel with an extensive food selection. We're in Mexico, for crying out loud. Why do you need Subway, Jaivon? I'm walking into the store on the main street, and I freeze in my tracks when I hear Jaivon screaming and throwing his jacket at Mommy. No. Freaking. Way. This cannot be happening. Not now, on our tropical vacation in Mexico. Now, when you picture this in your head, I don't want you to think of a toddler throwing a fit and screaming because his mom told him no. This was no "cute" temper tantrum that gets resolved with a quick "pop" or buying the kid a popsicle. I want you to imagine a fully grown black man in his twenties raging out in the streets and screaming, cursing, and being violent. He's throwing things, cursing, yelling, "I DON'T LIKE YOU, MOMMY." He probably threw a "FUCK YOU BITCH" in there. He probably threw a "YOU'RE A FUCKING BITCH MOMMY" in there. "I DON'T LIKE YOU MOMMY." "DON'T LOOK AT ME DOMINIQUE." Those were his standard lines.

Everyone on the main street in Mexico is looking at the three of us, shocked. I'm feeling a mix of emotions right now: fear, anxiety, embarrassment, and worry. Are the police about to come and shoot this crazy black man who happens to be my brother? I look out into what was a peaceful crowd of tourists and see everyone just staring at all of us. Quite frankly, at this point, I am trying to avoid eye contact with every person that I see staring at us in disbelief. Why is Jaivon doing this? He never acts up in public! Why now? How could this happen after Mommy planned this memorable vacation for us? Why can't we have a regular family outing? A sense of normalcy amidst our abnormal circumstances. We turn the corner, and the police arrive, armed with guns drawn. Jaivon hadn't even been going on for ten minutes in his outrage, and the cops were already on the street waiting for us. My mom tells Jaivon to sit down, and he listens, THANK GOD.

My mom tells him to take his medicine, and he complies. Except, he's kind of not complying because he's spitting it out. He's spitting the pills out on the ground and then picking them back up to swallow them with water. This guy is losing it; oh my goodness. We're screwed. The cops are asking us what happened and would you believe it if I said not one of them spoke English! Shoot! I took Spanish at my school for about a year at the time. I was translating to them that Jaivon was my brother. My mom got my grandmother on the phone since she speaks a clean amount of Spanish. My grandma told my mom to tell the police that he was "loco." My mom just kept saying, "Loco, loco, loco." Loco means CRAZY.

At that point, Jaivon officially ruined our vacation. So thankfully after what felt like forever, Jaivon pulled it together, and we went back to the hotel. But the vibe was killed. The mood was dead. Jaivon ruined our trip to Mexico. I hated this for us, especially for my mom. That woman right there has been through so much with my brother. And that happened to be the breaking point for her. Jaivon can no longer live with us. He's too dangerous. It was time to leave Mexico and come back home, and Mommy and I were praying that Jaivon wouldn't decide to start turning up at the airport. At that point, if he chose to act up there, we might not make it out of Mexico together. If Jaivon acts up at the airport, he will either get shot or locked up in Mexico's prison, and we do not want either of the two to happen.

We were all checked in, waiting to board our flight, when Jaivon decided that he needed a port to plug his phone into. He's walking around trying to find a port, and we can sense that his behavior is still a bit off. We can feel it in our stomachs. That's what trauma has done to us over the years. It has given us this feeling of rising anxiety and the ability to sense a brewing earthquake. Fortunately, we made it home in one piece without a part two of what happened on the main street. Now, it's game time, and Mommy has to find a different housing option for Jaivon. This trip was a wake-up call, and immediate action was needed for the safety of all of us.

Chapter 11

Mommy

The woman that Jaivon and I call 'mommy' is a warrior. She made me aware that not only is Jaivon autistic, but he also has bipolar disorder. This diagnosis makes perfect sense, considering he can be perfectly fine at 5:00 and then have an outburst at 5:30 pm. Nonetheless, that's not what this chapter is about. This chapter is about Rhonda Jennifer. My mom noticed my brother's abnormal behaviors, such as rocking and head banging, when he was a toddler. His speech was delayed, and he began speaking in complete sentences at the age of five. She found out that Jaivon was autistic when he was two years old. From what I heard, he was a handful as a child. The schools used to call her all the time while she was at work to report every little thing that Jaivon did. "Jaivon took off his shoes!"

Now that I have a child of my own, I realize that this must be overwhelming. Mommy never wanted to hurt Jaivon, even when he was unstable and raging out of control. He would run up on her, and truthfully, she'd take it like a champ. Her thought process is, "he has a mental illness; it wouldn't be right to hurt him." However, I recall her giving him that good molly wop in our basement one time. Only once. But one time was all I needed from her. His aide, Kenny, and I were so proud of her at the time. Mommy finally fought back, and at the time, it was a huge win. Fast forward to his adult years, Jaivon still needs support. When you have a child with special needs, you don't just send them to college and then count on them to get married and move out and be out of your care. You are always. Caring. For. This. Person. My mom is Jaivon's permanent caregiver. I know this is a tiring job for Mommy. I know it comes with a roller coaster of emotions, but she takes it like a champ. Did I mention she's also a breast cancer survivor?

I saw tubes of blood hanging from my mommy's stomach when she was in the recovery process. She had her breasts removed with a double mastectomy. Yet, she still made sure that Jaivon and I were taken care of. We never missed a meal or a day of school. Even when Mommy was down, she made sure that our lives were never on pause. The way she loves Jaivon is truly unconditional. After all of the fuck you's and fuck you bitches, I don't know how many other mothers would do the things that Mommy does for Jaivon. I wonder if she's ever wanted to give up and say screw it. But she has never done that.

Mommy, if you're reading this, I take my hat, sweater, and shirt off to you. I salute you, Mommy. I thank you for being all that and a bag of chips for Jaivon and me. Thank you for never missing a beat. You have taught me resilience and the importance of forging forward. The amount of mercy and patience that you have exhibited throughout Jaivon's life is impeccable. You have shown me the true definition of unconditional love that a mother has for their child. You have demonstrated real love through the most trying circumstances.

Chapter 12

The First and Last Group Home

After the Mexico fiasco, Mommy knew that Jaivon was officially too dangerous to be under the same roof as us. His explosions were always confined to the four walls of our household. Before Mexico, Jaivon had NEVER acted out in public. Mommy searched and searched and searched her heart out for a group home for him. Now, putting your son in a group home is a heartbreaking decision. It was her last resort. Imagine sending the son that you are supposed to love and protect to a group home to live with other people who are also on the spectrum or, worse, severely retarded. But that's just what mommy was doing it for: to love and protect him from himself.

My great-uncle Cloudy lives in Jamaica and was willing to take Jaivon under his wing for two whole weeks while Mommy figured things out. It was a blessing to have family members who were always willing to step in and help. Even at the time of Jaivon's autism diagnosis as a toddler, my grandparents were living in Puerto Rico and packed up their lives to move back to Boston to help out. Two weeks later, Jaivon returned from Jamaica, and it was move-in day. It's bittersweet for all of us, to be honest. We knew it was the best decision and for the safety of all of us. Although, no one wanted to see Jaivon go. He's going from the nice suburbs with his family to a house with strangers—men whose parents either were deceased or couldn't take on the extra stress.

The group home had rotating staff throughout the day and night, so the men were in good hands. There was one man, Anthony, who would go around pinching people. I think he has pinched Jaivon a few times, and I won't lie, I found it humorous when he would tell us about this. Whenever we visited Jaivon at the group home, Anthony would be there, saying, "Have fun with that!" for no apparent reason. You could be speaking with him, and he'll respond with, "Have fun with that!" Here's the thing about group homes:

they are government-funded, and the income goes to the person in charge of the house. So, every involved parent or guardian hopes that they are not just in it for the money.

Mommy scoped this place out, and if that woman scopes a place out, she's looking at all of the ins and outs. She wasn't dropping him off and saying, "Have a good life."

She would still come and visit him very frequently, of course, because that's her only son. Not only did she want to see him, but she also wanted to ensure that things were running as they were supposed to. They promised my mom they'd take good care of him and maintain his usual routine. One of those promises was that they would take him skating weekly, which is something Jaivon loved and was very accustomed to. Fast forward, my mom goes to visit Jaivon, and his face is disheveled. No haircut, no beard trim. No skating outings. Broken promises. What in the world are these people doing? One day, she gets a call from my brother, who says they are showering out of buckets. Pause.

Many group home owners and workers count on the fact that the people living there are either nonverbal, retarded, or incompetent so that they can just get away with unethical behavior. Unfortunately for them, but fortunate for us, Jaivon is none of the above. He knows and understands very well what it means not to have water in the house. When I say, Mommy was infuriated! At this point, Mommy had decided that a group home was not the right place for Jaivon, and she moved him out of there immediately. But our home isn't the place for him either. So, between talking with some workers from his agency and his behavior specialist, they decided on a host home. Oh, and did I mention Mommy reported the group home to the state? She built an entire case.

Chapter 13

The First and Last Host Home

Jaivon coming back to live with Mommy and me was not an option. Mexico proved that he was a danger not only to us but to the public at large. After a thorough search, she found Mr. and Mrs. Evans—a beautiful, older couple with a home that had room for two mentally disabled adults. Essentially, host homes consist of single families that host adults with mental illness. Mr. and Mrs. Evans had a lovely home and were from Jamaica. They had one other young man, Landon-Earl, who was already living with them. Landon-Earl's mom passed away, so he didn't have a parent coming to check in on him. However, the Evans family was so trustworthy that he was fine without his immediate family constantly looking for him. He was a taciturn young man, yet still able to take care of himself.

This house was the perfect fit for Jaivon.

Fast forward, he's getting home-cooked meals every day. I'm talking about home-cooked Jamaican meals every day. He landed a job at Dunkin' Donuts, about five minutes away from the house, and was living a great life. Jaivon had it made at this house. Mommy, of course, would go and visit Jaivon and check in on him. He was always wonderful when she saw him and talked to him on the phone. He even had his own room! The Evans were still in their honeymoon phase with Jaivon. He hadn't exposed his dark side to them yet. Until he did. My mom gets a phone call that Jaivon has exploded and physically attacked Mr. Evans, the man of the house. He was left with bleeding scratches all over his bald head. I'm sure you can guess what comes next: After a great year, Jaivon has to leave the host home.

This was disheartening for Mommy because the Evans family was such an excellent fit for Jaivon. She felt like she had finally hit the jackpot for him, and she truly did. Now, it's time for another game plan. Another group home? No. Come back to live with us? Hell no. Jaivon living with us is too anxiety-provoking. Once he gets in his unstable state and we know he's about to blow his top, we're walking on eggshells, just waiting for it to happen. I mean, stomachs turning and preparing for impact. However, Mommy has always been quick on her feet. She's impulsive but in a significant way. The type of person who will say she's doing something, and she will have it completed that same day. She thinks her decisions through, but it doesn't usually take her super long to think them through. These impulsive decisions are some of her best decisions. They keep her up at night, and she doesn't sleep until the plan is entirely carried out. Once everything is settled, Mommy can finally rest at night. Finally, Mommy decided to switch up what has been regular for Jaivon's entire life. She decided to buy Jaivon his own house. There is no host family, no group home staff, just Jaivon.

Chapter 14

Cloudy Mill Lane

There was a house located on Cloudy Mill Lane for sale on Zillow that needed some fixing up. The price was too reasonable just to pass up, and it was only a five-minute commute from Mommy's house; of course, she purchased it. She flew in a close family friend who does renovations to complete the upgrades of Jaivon's house. They did a beautiful job, and the house truly looked brand new. The house was a complete 180 when it was finished being renovated. When Mommy has a vision for a home, she knows how to bring it to life. She has years of experience in real estate investing and owns multiple properties. She's just that boss lady!

Jaivon was very excited about the idea of having his own house. The house consists of three bedrooms and two bathrooms. There's a beautiful backyard, a carport outside, a spacious living room, and, of course, a kitchen. The kitchen wall was cut with a square in the middle during the renovations so that the person who's cooking can see out into the living room.

Mommy has always been a planner. She always will be. I know her biggest fear is the well-being of Jaivon if she passes away. She wants Jaivon to be set up so that God forbid if she dies, he has his own home that no one can throw him out of amid his episodes. In a host home, he's liable to attack the owners and get kicked out. In a group home, he's liable to attack anyone and even potentially not receive the best care. She never wanted to see him rotting away in a group home. Or, you know, bathing out of a bucket. So, house it was. Now, Jaivon is set up for success. He has aides who come to his house daily, and he still experiences violent earthquakes. It sucks to think about death and plan for the worst. However, families often become lost when they lose the anchor of their family because they are not being correctly set up by the person who passed. Mommy wants to know that Jaivon will be fully taken care of and in good hands if the Lord decides it's time for her to leave this earth.

Back at our childhood home, my mom never wanted to utilize the police as a source of help during Jaivon's episodes because there was always a risk that they could harm him for his violent behavior. Once Jaivon moved to Cloudy Mill Lane, Mommy decided to take Jaivon to the Police Precinct to meet the Chief of the police in the area, along with multiple officers. She made them aware of his condition and informed them that he lives alone. The team at the precinct was all very receptive and welcoming to Jaivon. They even took photos at the end of the meeting. Mommy even informed all of his neighbors about his condition and gave them her contact information in case an emergency occurred. She always goes the extra mile to ensure that Jaivon is protected when he has his outbursts.

The beautiful thing about Jaivon living alone is that Mommy can manage him from afar. She only lives five minutes away, which makes it easier for her to check on him at any time. She can pop in on him and his aides, cook for him sometimes, and be there to meet his needs. If he's in one of his moments, she can choose not to go over there. I love the freedom that this has brought her. Back when Jaivon was living at home, we had no choice but to deal with his earthquakes and the anxiety that came with them. Finding great aides has always been a hassle, but thankfully, he currently has two great, reliable ones. But he hasn't always.

The House Aides on Cloudy Mill Lane:

My mom didn't want Jaivon to be alone every day, so she maintained a routine of having aides with him daily to help out and ensure he was alright. They'd take him to work, help him cook and prepare his meals, and be an extra set of eyes for my mother. Honestly, the aides were also there for the company, although he didn't always want the company to be there.

Stella: Stella was one of the first aides who started coming to Jaivon's new house. She was terrible. There are no other words to describe her. Well, I have one that may suffice: unprofessional. The agency providing the aides seemed to be hiring just anybody, from the looks of it. Their pay wasn't all that high either, so of course, the quality of people wasn't that great. For starters, Mommy had cameras in the house, and thank God she did. Mommy looks at the camera and sees Stella taking naps on the couch almost every day. She was the type of employee that you can tell stories about, and the person hearing you will ask if you're joking. This was no joke. She would sleep in the same corner of the couch almost every day. Let me not forget to mention that she put plastic in the microwave and burned it. That was the end of her. Stella, you're fired, honey!

Karlita: Karlita was a family friend of my mom's aunt. She became employed with the agency and started working with Jaivon. Jaivon loved working with her, especially in their honeymoon phase. My mom was fond of having some sort of familiarity with her since she was a family friend. One problem, though: Karlita didn't have a car. It's ironic, considering her name is Kar-lita. My mom, at the time, had two vehicles: a van and a Jeep. The van wasn't being used, so out of the kindness of her heart, she would let Karlita use the vehicle to transport Jaivon to and from work and also to take him skating. This was lovely until my mom realized that the van was gone during hours that Karlita was not working. Gone overnight. My mom lives about five minutes from Jaivon, so driving over there is no challenging task. She went over there one night and saw that the van being gone was becoming a pattern. Now, this is just inappropriate. She wasn't even offering to pay for gas to cover her driving. Mommy confronted Karlita about it, and furthermore, Karlita quit. Thanks for nothing, Karlita. Now Jaivon's anxious that he doesn't have an aide, Mommy is worried that he's on edge, and you got to walk in here and have a free car for a few weeks. Karlita, you may be gone, but certainly not forgotten!

Big Al: Big Al was a good house aide for Jaivon. Jaivon has a thing with male aides, though. He prefers to work with women because he wants to be coddled and get away with all the sugar, honey, and iced tea in the world. So, big Al had a pretty good run with Jaivon. He wasn't babying him, to my knowledge. One day, Jaivon had a doctor's appointment, and Big Al drove him to it. For some reason, Mommy and I met them there. Things were going fine until we got off the elevator to go back to our cars. Jaivon starts flipping out in the parking lot, and I can't even remember why, but he is going crazy on Big Al. Screaming at the top of his lungs, mind you, we are in public. I wish this guy would stop embarrassing us in public with his psychotic outbreaks. Big Al is probably between 300 and 400 pounds. At the time, Jaivon was about a good 190, maybe 200 pounds. Jaivon runs up to Big Al, and he hits his chest repeatedly. Big Al stands there and looks at him like he's a child. Because he is truly acting like one. But here's Jaivon with all of his force, just hitting on this man's chest with both of his hands. Banging on him as if he's beating a drum. Big Al didn't even move a centimeter. His weight worked in his favor. Then, Jaivon continues fuming and starts going on about how he doesn't like Big Al and doesn't want him to drive him home. In my head, I'm thinking, "There's no way he's about to ride home with us like this."

He starts banging on the windows of Big Al's car with all of his might. I mean banging HARD with both hands. At this point, he must want to break the windows of this man's car. My mom is in the background shouting, "Jaivon, no!" But he keeps pounding on this man's car. Big Al could've roughed him up if he wanted to, but he chose not to. Humble guy. But he should've. Jaivon ended up riding home with us and I was sitting in the front, literally just hoping he wouldn't blow his top in the car. Thankfully, the car ride home wasn't eventful. Big Al, I'm just glad that you were physically built to withstand the earthquake of Jaivon. Again, it is time for a new aide.

Lauren: (present-day)

Lauren currently works with Jaivon at his house; however, she is starting to get on his bad side. She didn't do anything to Jaivon in particular; Jaivon has an expiration date with certain people. I do wonder if his aides have certain behaviors that may trigger him or leave a bad taste in his mouth. Maybe there's a chance that there is a reason for all of their expiration dates with him. Lauren's time is almost up with him, and we can all see it. When she comes to take him to work, he does not answer the door for her. This is Lauren's job; she has to go and take Jaivon to work and assist him with any needs in his daily routine, and Jaivon won't open the door for her. They are heading out to the park, and he shouts, "LEAVE ME ALONE," and swings at her. Once Jaivon decides that he no longer wants an aide working with him, it puts Mommy in a bind because not only does she employ the aides, but they also take him to work. So when Jaivon decides not to let Lauren in for work, Mommy is still left to pay her for a full shift that she could not work, and Jaivon has missed out on yet another day of work. Thankfully, Lauren has experience working with people similar to Jaivon, and this is not her first time navigating such situations. It is very admirable of her to continue working somewhere that is becoming increasingly challenging with every shift. Not knowing whether your client will be happy, sad, or upset is likely very anxiety-provoking, I am sure. Lauren, you have been great, and as much as we hope that you continue with Jaivon, we don't blame you for leaving.

Kim and Sprocket

These were our dogs, who kept Jaivon's company at his home, and they gave him a sense of purpose. He was responsible for taking them outside, replenishing their water, and feeding them daily. Things were great until they weren't. Kim was our childhood dog, and she started to show signs of aging. Her bowels were getting looser, and she wasn't able to control them. She started having a good number of accidents around the house, which was just frustrating for Jaivon. Whenever she peed or pooped around the house he needed to clean it up.

Sprocket was the dog that we got after the passing of our first dog, Chowder. Together, Kim and Sprocket were a pivotal part of Jaivon's life. There's nothing like coming home to furry friends wagging their tails, excited to see you. Or going to sleep knowing that if a stranger walks up to the house, the dogs will bark at the top of their lungs to alert you. Jaivon started to take out his aggression on the dogs. He never seriously hurt them, thankfully, but he did hit poor Sprocket out of anger. Sprocket was not having it and as a response, he bit Jaivon. Good for Sprocket. I spoke to Jaivon on the phone after this, and when he told me that Sprocket bit him, I said, "Good. That will teach you not to hit him". There are times when I find it difficult to believe I have to say certain things to my brother. Having to tell him that he shouldn't hit the dog out of anger is ludicrous to me. Kim is no longer with us; may she rest in peace. Sprocket has a new family, and his neediness became too much for Jaivon to handle. He's a happy dog, though, and is happier with his new family eating homemade peanut butter cake and sleeping in their beds.

Chapter 15

Car Attacks

You read that right. When Jaivon is mentally unstable and he's having a violent outburst, you're liable to be attacked. And when he's unstable in a vehicle, buckle up. Or maybe I should say unbuckle and get as far away from the car as possible. The amount of uneasiness that Mommy and I would feel in the car with him when his mood started to take a turn cannot be described. There were times when we would be riding around on eggshells, just hoping and praying that he would not flip in the car. I would be just praying to make it home safely, all of us in one piece.

I remember he was about fourteen when he tried to jump out of the car when Mommy was driving. We are already on edge and anxious when his mood starts to shift, and we can see that he is getting ready for one of his not-so-amazing days. But when that happens in the car, it's nerve-wracking. I don't say this to make light of Jaivon's condition at all; I say it to give you a visual. Imagine being in the car with a psycho who is only seeing red for a moment. I've ridden in the car when Jaivon has been unstable, but thankfully, he has never attacked Mommy while she was driving. That was always a fear of mine. What if he attacks her? What if he makes her crash the car? Of course, what if he attacks me has come to mind, but I never seriously entertained the thought because it has never happened, even to this day. He knows better. Daddy wouldn't have it, and Jaivon knows that.

His most recent car attack took place this year, actually, in 2025. My grandparents were in town after my husband, Nate, and I had our first child. It was on this day that we decided to have a family dinner, and Nate and I hosted. My anxiety was a bit triggered because although Jaivon is normally stable when family surrounds him, I had an infant at home. My son was only a couple of months old at the time. I hate the intrusive thoughts, but they do come. All I could see was Jaivon picking him up and chucking him at the fireplace. Lord have mercy. These are very dark, intrusive thoughts, but the trauma will make you have those. I was calling my husband and texting him to check in. No, I didn't tell him at the time I was worried about Jaivon because I knew that he wouldn't let anything happen to him. Fortunately, everything remained peaceful throughout the entire day. Jaivon held him, we got pictures, and we had a great dinner.

On the menu, bread was a side. Now, Mommy has Jaivon on a gluten-free diet because she has noticed over the past few years that there is a correlation between his outbursts and gluten. So, Jaivon was disappointed that he couldn't have any bread. He didn't act out, though, and he didn't seem to be getting unstable. He left our house perfectly fine. Or at least it appeared that he was perfectly fine.

We ended the dinner on a great note, and they drove off to head back to Mommy's house. Until Mommy shows up at the door, looking distressed. She left her phone at our house and needed to come back for it. She told us, "Jaivon is in the car screaming, FUCK YOU MOMMY, YOU'RE A FUCKING BITCH MOMMY". She said she told him to run into the house and get her phone for her, and he started going off, screaming those terrible things. This is one of those moments when I ask myself why he's doing this after such a lovely family day. I am wondering how he was perfectly fine less than ten minutes ago when they all got in the car to leave. Him switching his mood in such a quick instant is something that you can only understand if you've witnessed it. It puts everyone around him on edge not knowing what sort of destruction he's going to do, and who he can potentially hurt this time. Mind you, the vehicle consists of my mom, Jaivon, and my grandparents.

Half of me hates that this is happening. The other half is glad that my grandparents get to witness this behavior. Now, I'm not saying I'm so happy they're seeing this as if I'm walking around parading it. I don't want them to be injured. You have to understand they have painted this false image of Jaivon for YEARS. They've heard of his outbursts and may have even heard him yell a little bit. But they have never seen a showdown, let alone one that's happening in a moving vehicle. I wanted them to physically see a showdown with their own eyes so they could have a visual of what we're saying is happening. Although, I have to say that I hate that the earthquake that they're witnessing is in the car. They will more than likely be traumatized. We all are at this point.

Anywho, my mom drives off, and they head home. Thirty-minute drive home, with Jaivon, mentally unstable, blazing with anger in the back of the car, sitting across from my grandpa. My grandma took the front seat. Thank God. Although, I don't see him ever attacking her. Jaivon has a way with people, and he knows who not to touch. Then again, he's super unpredictable, and anyone can get it. Sitting in the living room, my dad, Nate, and I are just hoping they get home safely. My stomach is in knots, twisting and turning. My hands are trembling with the amount of nervousness I'm feeling right now. Suddenly, my dad's phone rings and I look over and see Jaivon's name appear across the screen. Goodness.

"Hey, Ta".

"Hey J, how you doin'?"

"Not too good. I just had an outburst".

They proceed to continue conversing, and out of nowhere, mid-conversation, "I HATE YOU, GRANDPA, FUCK YOU GRANDPA! I DON'T LIKE YOU". I can hear my mom in the background telling Jaivon to calm down, but there's no stopping him. We hear a bunch of shuffling in the car, and my heart is beating ninety miles per minute. I'm just thinking oh my goodness, please don't crash this car. Finally, it stops.

Silence. Mommy pulls the car over. My dad proceeds to continue the conversation:

"J, are you there? You good?"

"I hit my Grandpa".

"Why did you do that?"

"I didn't know it was gonna happen. I didn't know I was gonna do that. I didn't know this was gonna happen today".

Pause.

Now, that is some scary stuff. What do you mean you didn't know you were gonna do that, Jaivon?

Daddy stays on the phone with Jaivon until they get home. Jaivon tells Daddy that he broke my grandfather's glasses and hit him. He said that my grandfather told him he was afraid of him. Daddy tries speaking with Jaivon about a lighter topic, and I quietly say to him in the background that he should stay on the phone with him until they get home because I know it would make Mommy feel more comfortable. It's wild how in tune my mom and I are during Jaivon's earthquakes because a minute later, Daddy gets a text from her asking him to stay on the phone with her. Daddy and Jaivon start talking about music, and I hear Jaivon singing one of the songs that they were discussing. He sounds wacko.

He went from screaming and cursing, attacking my grandfather in the backseat of the car, to now singing. Jaivon's psychotic breaks are very crazy to witness and even more crazy to hear over the phone. I do have a few thoughts about this car ride: Now, Grandpa, why would you 1). Tell this man you are afraid of him to give him an upper leg? He's liable to do this again, and now that you're "afraid," he won't think twice about it! 2). Did you sit there and let Jaivon beat you up in a moving car? I mean, I know it caught him off guard, but he should've popped him in the head, mouth, or something! You sat there and got attacked in the car without putting up any kind of defense. I cannot fathom this. Well, I can, but I should say I wish my grandpa had used self-defense. Now the "oh, he has a mental illness" excuse is out the window. You are attacking someone in a moving car; you need to be corrected pronto.

So, let's establish some ground rules with Jaivon:

Rule Number 1: NEVER take a drive that's more than twenty minutes with him. If he starts getting unstable, at least you're somewhat close to home, and hopefully, he can keep it contained.

Rule Number 2: NEVER let him attack without a hit back. He NEEDS to feel some physical response. You don't have to give him a black eye; treat him the way you would treat any grown adult that is attacking you. Goodness, I just want people to treat him normally.

Rule Number 3: NEVER show that you're afraid. He can sense fear.

Chapter 16

The Abnormalities

Bubbles. "NO, GET IT AWAY FROM ME!" He'd shout when he saw any water toy. I have no idea why he is terrified of these, but he is. Those snow globes in the store that you can shake up and the snow expands scare the life out of him. Any bubbles, either in a bottle or even in a kids' toy, frighten him. I would use this for good laughs at times. I knew he was afraid, and as his little sister, I just wanted to mess with him. Sometimes, I would even act like I had bubbles behind my back to get a rouse out of him for fun. My mom or grandma would tell me to stop messing with him. When he realized I was joking about having bubbles behind my back, he would laugh it off with me. But when I had one of these terrorizing toys, he would run as far away from me as he could and tell me to stop. I always asked myself if he had a water trauma or something growing up, but he's fine with soap and water.

Yes, he takes showers; don't even think to ask yourself that. It's just the toys that trigger him. Grandma would keep the snow globe toys at the top of her shelf where he couldn't see them and where I couldn't reach them. I used to wonder if the bubbles could be used as a defense mechanism when he is attempting to attack someone. I wonder if Mommy could have kept a "bubbles" necklace on hand and just put it on when she felt him starting up to scare him off. Sometimes, Jaivon will drool a bit while he's talking, and it's just a side effect of the medications that he takes. He takes so much medication, oh my goodness. Not only is he on lots of meds, but he also gets an injection once a month that is supposed to keep him stabilized. I remember he had a Monday-Friday pill bottle that my mom would distribute all of his medicine into. I would see him open one of the tabs daily to take his medicine, and it was always so much per day. Mommy says without all of those meds, he'd be off the walls.

Jaivon stims by rocking. He will rock himself with head-phones on his ears, plugged into his CD player. This was a common sight that I would see through the crack of his door when his room was across from mine. I tried this myself one time to see what it's like, but I couldn't get into it. I remember sitting there, legs crisscrossed, putting my hands on my elbows like he would, and just rocking back and forth. Nothing. No satisfaction. He walks and talks perfectly fine. Although, when he does those things, the average person can see that something is off. He articulates well, and his speech is excellent; however, he sometimes drags out his words. "HEYYY DOMINIQUE" "HEYYY TA" "HOW YOU DOIN" His voice doesn't sound like that of a thirty-year-old. It's deep but not super mature in the way he articulates.

We shared a bathroom when we still lived together, and that meant sharing a tube of toothpaste. In our case, there were multiple tubes of toothpaste. Usually, when you squeeze the toothpaste out onto your toothbrush, you pinch it lightly, using a pincer graph (thumb and pointer finger). When I tell you, our toothpaste tubes would be so bent out of shape because he was squeezing them with his entire hand rather than just two fingers. That was his preferred method. At least we were both brushing our teeth. At some point, I didn't want to share a bathroom with him anymore, so I just ended up using Mommy's bathroom in the morning until Jaivon moved into the basement. At that point, the bathroom was all mine, both double sinks. When Jaivon walks, it is very significant to only him. He sticks out his belly slightly and has a slight bounce on his toes. He doesn't toe-walk, but when he walks, it is very evident when he is going onto his toes. He sways a bit from side to side, but it is no longer as apparent as he has lost a significant amount of weight. The weight loss looks great on him, and I am so happy for him. He looks healthier, and I'm sure he feels much lighter.

I've gotten over this now. But I would get this feeling as a child and even as a teenager when it was time to introduce Jaivon as my brother to a friend or acquaintance. I don't want to describe it as being ashamed or nervous. Maybe a good in-between. Sometimes, I would get it out of the way and tell them in advance that he's autistic so they're not left wondering when they meet him. Or I would just let them meet him without saying anything in advance and let it go as it goes. I won't say that I was embarrassed, but having to go through introductions with people who didn't already know his condition wasn't fun. We never went to the same school. He didn't attend the functions I was at. So how would they know unless I mentioned it or they came to my house?

I remember when my Sweet 16 was coming up, I had a conversation with my best friend about potentially just announcing that my brother is autistic so that people wouldn't make fun of him. He has a different way of dancing and just acting in general, so I didn't want him to be made fun of. I didn't want him to be a laughingstock. That was super dumb and childish. I hate that the thought even came to mind. But this book is a release of all of the things that I loved, hated, and experienced.

I look back and realize that if anyone were to do that, they shouldn't have been at the party anyway. I feel so stupid for even considering that. I put myself in his shoes and imagine hearing that announcement about myself. My mom kept him in a separate room for the night while my friends and peers all gathered in the party room. I wonder if she did this because she knew deep down how I felt or if she just wanted me to have the limelight without worrying about Jaivon. Maybe she did that as a 'just in case' he decided to act out (which would have been unusual for him at an event like this). There are people in school who would look astonished when I mentioned my brother. It's because Jaivon and I weren't the type of siblings that were always together. It wasn't a 'when you see him, you see me' kind of situation. It was quite the opposite. Many people didn't know I even had a brother. "You have a brother?" would be their response if I mention him. Some people will probably read this book and ask the same question: "You have a brother?" I re-member having a conversation with a girl who asked about my brother, inquiring about what he was like and if he was cute, and I became extremely uncomfortable. I didn't feel like explaining. Well, he's probably not your type because he's autistic and not mentally there all the way, and sometimes he explodes. Additionally, he rocks himself during the day and sometimes attacks my mom or his aides when he's not well. He calls my mom a bitch when he's angry and yells, "fuck you." That conversation was dead real quick.

As a child, I was navigating how to introduce my brother to people. When speaking to people about him, I sometimes wouldn't leave out that he was autistic. The adult me realized that I was putting a label on him and painting a picture of him for people that wasn't even necessary. Adult me isn't go-ing just voluntarily to state for fun that my brother is autis-tic. Instead, Adult me describes him as an adult who lives independently, has a steady job, and tends to keep to him-self. Adult me would not exclude him from a function or even think of it just because he's different. Well, maybe I'll exclude him for safety and peace of mind, as he now acts out in public. However, if he didn't, I wouldn't exclude him at all.

When I married my husband, our wedding reception was such a blast. We were swag surfing, dancing, turning up, and just having a great time. Jaivon was on the dance floor doing his thing. He was swag surfing with all of us and just having a great time. He's dancing, enjoying the loud music, and he's in an atmosphere that he loves. This brings me peace, knowing how comfortable I was with him there. It felt so normal. It didn't feel like everyone was dancing and doing their thing, and there was Jaivon off to the side, looking like a weirdo. It was normal. The thought never came to mind, "What if he looks off?" or "What if he gets laughed at?" Now, that is how things should have been at my Sweet 16. Jaivon is having a great time amongst our peers. But I've learned and grown. I've become more comfortable with his condition.

He's a gifted man with a condition, but that's not what defines him. Despite all of the abnormalities, they do not define who Jaivon is as a person. They don't determine his capabilities or his character. They are just facts about his mind that we have to live with.

The golf cart incident

I don't know if this is an abnormality because not every "normal" person has common sense. Common sense was lacking on this day. Jaivon was still living at home at the time, and he conjured up the idea to drive our golf cart. Jaivon had never successfully driven the golf cart alone or driven it at all. What on earth made him want to do this, I don't know, but he did. So, Jaivon puts the key in the golf cart and backs out. However, the garage door was closed. Dammit, Jaivon, you could've killed yourself! Don't you know that if you're backing out of a vehicle, you have to open the garage? Thank GOD he didn't go forward! I was at school when this happened. I know that when I came home, the outside of the garage was in shambles. Completely ruined and broken down. Mommy said that when she pulled up to the house, she thought someone had broken in. I know she was nervous. I will never be able to understand how and why that happened, but it did—just another thing to add to my crazy experience.

Chapter 17

Uncle Cloudy

The same Uncle Cloudy, who lives in Jamaica and kept Jaivon for two weeks when my mom was trying to figure out where to put him, is the one who almost had bleach poured on his clothes. There was a time when he had business to handle in Georgia, and he would come to stay at our house. He would lodge in the basement with Jaivon. He was starting to overstay his welcome, as the next few times he came to Georgia, Jaivon made it very clear that he did not want him in his personal space. It started with the bleach call. Jaivon called Uncle Cloudy to let him know that he would pour bleach on his clothes when he came to town. I wonder what made him choose bleach on the clothes, of all things to say, but hey, that's my brother. Our uncle got the memo loud and clear. He said, "I'm not sleeping down there so Jaivon can throw bleach on my clothes."

I remember sitting in the kitchen with my best friend, my mom, and Uncle Cloudy. Uncle Cloudy tells us that Jaivon left him a voice message on his phone and lets us hear it.

"Hey, Uncle Cloudy, I wanted to send you this song that makes me think of you." He hits play on the message that follows, which is apparently the song that makes Jaivon think of him. The song goes "fuck you, fuck you, fuck you, fuck you" over and over. It was safe to say that Jaivon was tired of Uncle Cloudy staying in his personal space when he came on vacation or for business. He never stayed down in the basement with him again, and when he comes to town, he doesn't stay the night at his house now either. He is not willing to risk bleach on his clothes.

Chapter 18

The Love of My Life

Whoever I married would have to have compassion for others, especially for my brother. Jaivon absolutely loves music, and my husband Nate shares the same passion. Nate makes beats in his spare time and is genuinely very talented at what he does. We arranged for him to have a beat-making session with Jaivon, and it melted my heart to see the way they interacted together. The way Nate was so patient in explaining what each term meant and helped my brother form his own beat was a reminder of one of the many reasons I love my husband. Together, we have taken Jaivon skating and on other outings. Jaivon watched how savvy Nate was with making beats, and Nate got to see how savvy Jaivon was on the wheels at the skating rink.

At the time, Nate didn't have much experience skating, but as we went out more and more, he started to develop a love for it. Similar to the kind that Jaivon has for it. I have moments when I feel a bit sorrowful about my brother's situation. Just thinking about the things my family has endured with him and even the things Jaivon deals with makes me sorrowful at times. Nate has been there to encourage me through those moments, and that is one of the many reasons why I love and appreciate him.

Chapter 19

The "R-word"

"Retard"

Pronounced re-tard.

"delay or hold back in terms of progress, development, or accomplishment" (Oxford Dictionary)

This term is often used out of ignorance by people playfully to one another. I'm not a fan of the word because my brother has mild retardation. The people that use this word don't take into consideration that there are actual retarded and slow people out there. Some are more severely retarded than others. Imagine what their parents deal with every day, having a retarded child. Yet people use it in a manner to describe someone as stupid, jokingly. Or even mock people that are actually retarded.

The amount of compassion that having Jaivon as a sibling has taught me is amazing. I NEVER made fun of the kids at school with special needs. Never talked or joked about them. I would see and hear them out in the hallway back when I was in elementary, middle, and high school. Sometimes they would make noises that I found to be different. I knew that they couldn't help that they were dissimilar from those around them. I never got down with other people that did make jokes about the kids that had special needs or ailments. I always knew that could be someone making fun of my brother. There are times in public when someone will do something the slightest bit off and they could be totally normal but I give them the benefit of the doubt. I find myself saying "They could have special needs". People don't consider others with special needs on a deep level unless they know someone personally that deals with it.

They make jokes about the "short bus", but mind you my brother rode that bus. He's not handicapped, thank God, and he is very verbal. But he still rode that bus to school every day. That short bus pulled up to our house every morning on time and transported him to school. I will say that I want schools to do a better job of creating all-inclusive environments for students like my brother. They are always pulled out of class into their own safe haven and not really given the opportunity to experience social skills on the same level that "normal" kids are able to. I do understand that some disabilities are more severe than others and require a smaller setting. Also, I do understand that in life, kids can be cruel. So I see both sides of the fence.

Chapter 20

He's Normal

Aside from the abnormalities, Jaivon is still a thirty year old man. God willing, he will only get older physically in age. He is still capable of more than some give him credit for. He is able to use all of his senses, cook, clean, go to the gym, go skating, go to the movies, and much more. He also loves food, but who doesn't? There are things that have triggered Jaivon that I realize as an adult would trigger me too. For example, when Aunt Cheryl and my grandparents come to town, they tend to pop up and surprise Jaivon. Yeah, it's cute and all to surprise someone, but don't come to my house without calling. I could be walking around naked.

That's just the reality of it. Jaivon may have special needs, but he's still a grown man that enjoys his privacy. Mommy often feels bad that he wants to spend a lot of time alone, but that is totally normal. There are people like that in this world that don't want to constantly be around people. They're called 'introverts'. Being around people for a long amount of time or even a short amount of time can be over-stimulating, especially for someone that is autistic. He has moments when he decides that he does not want to go in to work so he just doesn't let his aide inside to take him to work that day. Whoever Mommy arranged to take him to work on a day that he decides that he's not going just gets left out-side.

They get a free day to just go about their lives and not worry about transporting Jaivon. Now, we all get that feeling of wanting a break or even deciding to call in sick. However, Jaivon just handles it a bit differently. I have to say he is a bit more bold than most of us. I don't think I would just not go into work without any kind of notice to my boss but he's not thinking that way. Mommy is working on educating him on the "you don't work, you don't eat" concept. This is some-thing that all of us "normal" people have to learn. If you de-cide to just up and quit your job, or even miss a few days because you don't "feel" like working, it cuts into your bills. That's life for everyone above ground, disabled or not.

Jaivon gets excited when a new song comes on the radio, and he loves to play his music loud. I do the exact same thing. I may express that excitement a bit differently, but I am the same way as a young adult. He gets irritated when Mommy tells him he can't have certain foods. Mommy just wants to help him maintain his diet because he has gone overboard before and gained way too much weight. But Jaivon is still a grown man that has desires and needs that he wants to fulfill.

When he earns money, he wants to buy electronics, specifically headphones. He is just a grown man earning an honest living that wants to spend it on something he enjoys. Now, I am a whole grown adult with an Amazon spending addiction. That doesn't make me abnormal.

Sometimes, I wonder if we're all a little bit autistic. Are we all on the spectrum in some way shape or form? In the morning when I get up and I'm rushing, I tend to scratch my throat with my mouth and it makes a scratching noise on the outside. A constant ongoing noise that sometimes I don't realize I'm doing. I realized that it is an anxious tick that I have. The other day there were fruit flies in my kitchen and I just hear myself scratching my throat frivolously as I'm deep cleaning the kitchen. Am I lowkey stimming? Jaivon rocks, maybe he does that when he's anxious to calm him down. Maybe his rocking is my throat scratching. Daddy pinches his nose and blows in and out, making a strange noise with his ear. Is he stimming?

I say this to say that maybe Jaivon is not all that abnormal. I'm not in denial now, he's definitely got issues. But we can't label every single thing he does as part of his condition. So family, if you're coming to town please ask Jaivon if you can come over. The same way you ask me to come over. If you have the key to Jaivon's house, please knock before going inside. He could be walking around naked, or he could be minding his own business. Think about the things you would expect from the company. Think about the boundaries that are unspoken that you expect to be respected.

Chapter 21

Bear

Nate and I found out we were pregnant shortly after I landed my first teaching job. One of my most consistent prayers was that our little bear would be born normally. I was so anxious, just constantly wanting our baby to be normal and not have to go through the things that my mom has gone through. I would see children with disabilities in public, and it would be another reminder of how much I didn't want my son to have one. Growing up with a brother like Jaivon will make you experience those feelings. Nate and I desire to have more kids, and I just don't want any of our kids to have the sibling experience that I had. I want them to have a normal interaction experience. I want them to grow up and be super close and have regular conversations. I don't want to have to sit one of them down and explain to them that their brother is not normal in the same way that they are. Even after the bear was born and developing, I would look at little things he did and start worrying if he was autistic.

I remember he was rubbing his fingers together at one point (exploring texture), and banging his arm on his lap before (exploring movement). He has outgrown these things and is a toddler. I remember asking Nate why the bear was doing something and his response was "don't worry babe he's not autistic". He reminded me that even if he was, that's still our child that we love and are responsible for. It's all in the Lord's hands. We don't get to pick how things go for us. Especially when it comes to some of the circumstances of our children. To our knowledge, the bear is a perfectly normal baby boy and I thank God for him everyday.

I also believe that I have to trust the Lord's perfect will. I hope and pray that if the Lord blesses us with another little bear, that my anxiety can be eased by the fact that the Lord knows what's best for us. Jaivon was not supposed to be anyone else's child but my mom. My mom has never given up on Jaivon, and she never abandoned him. In fact, she does too much for him. Mommy has always made sure jaivon had a silver spoon in his mouth, along with resources that were fitting for him. She had him a part of organizations that I wanted to be in myself because they just looked so fun on the outside. He would go horseback riding, have these aids take him to fun activities, and he would even get to go on field trips with a group that he was a part of. She helped him to land wonderful jobs with benefits, and was always pushing him to take the next steps. Jaivon may have autism. He may be bipolar. He may have mild retardation. But at the end of the day, he is still a human being with regular behaviors, wants, and desires. He is my brother who I love and appreciate for who he is.

Epilogue

Speaking in the present, Jaivon is in a better mood today. He was spiraling yesterday and tends to do that when his injection is coming up. Jaivon still lives alone and is thriving in his own house. He still locks Lauren out of the house sometimes, and other times, he lets her in with no problem. I still deal with the emotions of feeling sorrowful about Jaivon's condition at times. But I also have very great days with Jaivon, and I cherish those. I hope that this book touched individuals who have siblings with a mental illness. I hope you feel understood. I hope that this book touched the parents of a child with special needs. I hope you feel relatable. Lastly, I hope that this book educates individuals who have no clue what this experience is like. I hope you gain compassion.

About the Author

Dominique Leonard is a young adult who lives with her husband and son in the state of Georgia. She currently works full-time as a Virtual High School Math Teacher and part-time as a Dance Teacher. She was raised by both her mom and dad, two present parents who were nothing but amazing. Her passions include God, Family, Dance, Teaching, and reading books! She hopes to spread awareness of mental illness, autism, and bipolar disorder through this book. Her goal is to touch the hearts of those who may be living in similar circumstances.

Keep up with Dominique:
Instagram: @domleonardauthor
Email: domleonardauthor@gmail.com

Letter to My Brother

Dear Jaivon,

Growing up with you was never easy. I always wanted to just play games and watch movies together like regular siblings would. You weren't that interested in doing those things with me. Instead, we listened to loud music together. We play the game of Uno together sometimes. To this day, we go and grab a bite to eat together sometimes. We call each other on the phone for regular check-ins, especially after it's been too long since we last spoke. Our bond isn't like the bond that my friends have with their siblings. It is quite different, but the bond is still there. You've made me realize that it's not always about what I want to do. I had to learn to be a selfless sister. You have a voice too, and it's important to listen to what your desires are. You've taught me to have compassion for others and put myself in their shoes. You are a great big brother, and I am blessed to know you.

Love, Dominique

Book Club Questions

1. Is there anyone who can relate to the feelings of not having someone who understands what it's like to have a family member with special needs
2. What are your thoughts on the "R-word"? Do you think that people should use it knowing that it can be a derogatory and offensive term? Is it okay to just use it playfully because those surrounding you know the intentions behind the joke? Can you liken it to racial slurs that certain ethnicities are given a "pass" to use
3. What are some pivotal moments within this book that have resonated with you as a reader
4. If you are a parent of a child, teenager, or adult that undergoes psychotic breaks, what strategies do you use to ease the situation
5. Should students with special needs be given the chance to participate in extracurricular activities alongside peers who are typically developing
6. Do parents owe it to their kids to explain to them if they have autism

Acknowledgements

First and foremost, I want to thank God for allowing me to put my thoughts into words and for always being there for our family during the trying times in my childhood. I want to thank my Husband and my Parents for being listening ears before, throughout, and after the process of writing this book. To my Mom, thank you for being there to make edits to every draft I sent you without hesitation. Without you, I would not have completed this in the time I did or had the resources to create it. I get my sticktoitiveness from you.

To my little bear, thank you for reminding me what a mother's love truly means. Thank you to everyone who encouraged me to pursue my vision of writing this book. To Nicole Hicks, thank you for completing the publishing process and copyright registration for me, formatting my book for publication, and assisting with my cover design. I am beyond grateful for this experience and for everyone who accompanied me on the ride. To my childhood friends who came over to our home and never made me feel abnormal for living with a brother like Jaivon, thank you.